PENGUIN BOOKS

DEPTH OF FIELD

Desmond Francis Xavier Kon (Zhicheng-Mingdé) is the author of an epistolary novel, a quasi-memoir, two lyric essay monographs, four hybrid works, nine poetry collections, and this creative guided journal. A former journalist, he has edited more than twenty books and co-produced three audio books, several pro bono for non-profit organizations.

Trained in book publishing at Stanford University, Desmond studied sociology and mass communication at the National University of Singapore, and later received his theology masters (world religions) from Harvard University and fine arts masters (creative writing) from the University of Notre Dame.

In addition to grants from the National Arts Council and Singapore International Foundation, Desmond has enjoyed literary appointments at the Notre Dame Poetry Fellowship, NAC Gardens by the Bay Writing Residency, and NTU-NAC Creative Writing Residency.

Among other accolades, Desmond is the recipient of the IBPA Benjamin Franklin Award, Independent Publisher Book Award, National Indie Excellence Book Award, Poetry World Cup, Singapore Literature Prize, two Beverly Hills International Book Awards, and three Living Now Book Awards.

Praise for *Depth of Field*

'In this compelling book, Desmond Kon engages the reader in writing prompts that advance wellness and serve as an affirmation that the road to self-recovery exists. For those who question their own resilience and capacity to cope with life's challenges, this intricately designed book offers a path to a better world, regardless of whether one reflects on personal blemishes or sacred keepsakes. As the author astutely suggests, the key to success lies within.'

—Carolyn Kreiter-Foronda, PhD
Virginia Poet Laureate Emerita

'Desmond Kon's *Depth of Field: My Guided Journal for Self Healing* presents a beautiful opportunity for anyone who would like to draft letters to his or her essential self. This strikingly illustrated journal book asks us to make use of writing prompts to express who we are, have been, and might be someday. Kon plays with and against proverbial wisdom— frequently invoking fables and fairy tales with a special emphasis on *Aesop's Fables.* His prompts frequently suggest to users of the journal that they may want to tweak or even turn against traditional wisdom as they endeavor to achieve self-discovery. Kon—with his training in theology, creative writing, and book publishing—has made use of his many talents in the construction of *Depth of Field*, a journal book that can reveal a self to a self.'

—Joseph Stanton, PhD
Recipient of the Cades Award for Literature and
the Ka Palapala Poʻokela Award for Excellence in Literature

'*Depth of Field* is no literature: it's a godsend of good fortune and favour. Desmond Kon proves here poets can still be miracle workers and help people heal with word combinations. A kind of psycho-Orphism underlies the fables the author delicately sets up for us, to which responses are intended to be given through a dedicated space: each page opens a different landscape of your unconscious inland and moves smoothly its inhabitants—the wonder trees, farm animals and wild beasts of the mind. Genuinely empathetic and elegantly crafted, *Depth of Field* is an ardent invitation to become the poet of one's own life.'

—Pierre Vinclair, PhD
Recipient of the Académie Française Heredia Prize
and the Villa Kujoyama in Literature

'*Depth of Field* is a guided journal about kindness to self. It is full of delicious metaphors, allegories, imageries, and beautiful wordplay by a consummate wordsmith. It connects you to familiar fables playfully reinterpreted to respond to the existential angst we experience today. Above all, it delights your being in a reflective way—your eyes with its visual beauty, your mind with its intellectual stimulation, your heart with its colourful imagination and your will with its compelling analogies to nudge you to be kind to yourself by willing into being your true submerged self—simply by writing your reflections from the looking glass.'

—William Wan, PhD
General Secretary of the Singapore Kindness Movement
and Recipient of the President's Philanthropy and
Volunteerism Award

'*Depth of Field* performs the double task of providing self-help and overcoming writer's block during pandemic lockdowns and beyond. It provides an easy-to-follow literary approach to free writing, a key tool in overcoming trauma. It also promises to free oneself from any writing rut with exciting prompts. The illustrations and photos are gorgeous as we have come to expect from Desmond F. X. Kon Zhicheng-Mingdé. This is an inspirational book for our time.'

—Eric Tinsay Valles, PhD
Director of Poetry Festival Singapore
and Recipient of the Goh Sin Tub Creative Writing Prize

'*Depth of Field* is a rare work that has subtly and skilfully combined poetry and philosophy within the form of a self-help and activity book. The prompts—clearly the product of a mind and heart that lives with keen awareness and mindfulness—at once surprises, delights and provokes. These are prompts that will guide the reader to plumb the depths of the heart and scale the heights of the imagination that he/she/they would not have thought possible. This is a book that would not only heal. Its questions will open another world for you after which, you will not look at life you once knew the same again. It is a book that will make you look into yourself and find the gem within you that is waiting to be shared.'

—Phan Ming Yen
Fictionist and CEO of Global Cultural Alliance

'A whimsical activity book for grown-ups who need an escape from drudgery into wonderland. Follow Desmond down this perfectly-plotted rabbit hole—you'll find wild flights of imagination before coming face to face with yourself in meditative moments of clarity.'

—Amanda Chong
Co-Founder of ReadAble and
Recipient of the Singapore Youth Award

'During uncertain times, how vital it is to engage in the healing work of reflection. *Depth of Field* provides much-needed affirmation and consolation through insightful meditations of the mind and spirit. With tender precision, Desmond Kon has crafted a wise medley of enchanting creative exercises, akin to a recipe book for the heart. Let these imaginative prompts allow for pearls of experience to coalesce and crystallize, enacting and realizing all at once what the poet Mary Oliver has called "instructions for living a life".'

—Ow Yeong Wai Kit
Anthologist and Recipient of the Ministry of Education
Outstanding Youth in Education Award

'*Depth of Field* is a book about us and the stories we tell ourselves. Each journal prompt is simple yet profound, bearing the whimsical qualities of a fairy tale, with stories awaiting to be written by you, the reader. Intricately interwoven with *Aesop's Fables* along with ekphrastic elements to inspire imagination and contemplation, this journal is an invitation for us to look deeper and discover that healing begins within.'

—Nicole Kay
Founder of the Tapestry Project Singapore

DEPTH
OF
FIELD

MY
GUIDED JOURNAL
FOR
SELF HEALING

DESMOND KON

PENGUIN BOOKS

An imprint of Penguin Random House

PENGUIN BOOKS

USA | Canada | UK | Ireland | Australia
New Zealand | India | South Africa | China | Southeast Asia

Penguin Books is part of the Penguin Random House group of companies
whose addresses can be found at global.penguinrandomhouse.com

Published by Penguin Random House SEA Pte Ltd
9, Changi South Street 3, Level 08-01,
Singapore 486361

First published in Penguin Books by Penguin Random House SEA 2021

Copyright © Desmond Kon 2021

ISBN 9789814954662

www.penguin.sg

CONTENTS

I identify myself in language, but only by losing myself in it like an object. What is realized in my history is not the past definite of what was, since it is no more, or even the present perfect of what has been in what I am, but the future anterior of what I shall have been for what I am in the process of becoming.

Jacques Lacan

INTRODUCTION

'To pay attention,' Mary Oliver said, 'this is our endless and proper work.'

What does it take to pay attention to where we're at, what we've become—our present life station?

Depth of Field deftly combines the self-help book with the activity book. Framed by apothegms from Freud and Lacan, this book comprises 37 prime creative exercises, which may also be read as prompts or riddles. We discover well-loved fables within the Aesop tradition, both familiar and remote.

Accompanied with illustrations for ekphrastic inspiration, this book premises its ethos on the idea of writing as witness, investigating how writers engage with our personal history, and render particular experiences through the fine act of deeply felt writing.

What kinds of trauma, testimony and longing might find voice through such introspective narrative?

These prompts combine the powerful tools of narrative and Gestalt therapy. Through these fine-spun suggestions, the deep associative engagement approaches writing as a powerful means of healing. We find ourselves excavating long buried emotions and expressing them in such purposeful intimation.

Oliver herself recalls having a tough childhood, with a difficult family that brought with it a whole set of different problems. 'So I made a world out of words,' Oliver decided for herself. 'And it was my salvation.'

Indeed, the very act of writing can be deeply affecting, as much as the challenges life might throw our way. What we can choose to do is to carve out some time for ourselves, in order to think and feel more deeply about our own important lives, to invest in the beautiful act of writing to heal.

Through greater self-inquiry comes greater self-awareness, and thereby greater self-care.

The important thing is to 'write hard and clear about what hurts,' as Ernest Hemingway put it. Or, as William Wordsworth wrote: 'Fill your paper with the breathings of your heart.'

Depth of Field excellently speaks to the every person, from the adolescent to young adult, mature reader to retired elderly. The exercises work with such thoughtful complexity, so much so that they come across at once accessible and intellectual. The exercises are easy to read, yet compelling in their introspective scope. The prologue and epilogue, which sandwich the exercises, may serve up a deeper conceptual understanding of how the exercises may be approached.

Remember how much we loved those activity books as kids?

Depth of Field is reminiscent of just those activity books, filled with games and puzzles that encourage meaningful, self-initiated play. In the same manner in which such books kept us occupied and entertained, this guide is meant to be immersive. Each prompt helps the reader to explore some aspect of the self, mining deep memories, emotions and values.

What we write is completely up to us. We can attempt any genre, whether it's memoir, poetry, fiction or creative nonfiction. What remains important is that we reacquaint with our inner selves, developing a deeper sense of where we are in our life journey.

Indeed, this can all be as moving and ameliorating as a spiritual exercise.

Again, as Oliver would have wisely articulated it: 'So this is how you swim inward. So this is how you flow outwards. So this is how you pray.'

This is Dr Eichelberger's preamble.

It is a letter written especially for you.

This is Dr Eichelberger's prelude to a fable.
The fable is a peculiar, eccentric space.
It is at once a house of mirrors,
and a quaint house of curiosities.

Aesop is in the room. He leans by the painting.
Beside him are his animal friends.
The fox is seated on one end of Freud's couch.
The tortoise is asleep, at the edge of the carpet.
The hare rests on the teak mantel.

This is a safe space, where all are welcome.
Here, every manner of thing—truth, fiction,
memory, history, anecdote, myth, poem, story—
sits comfortably, next to one another.

Here will be written a fable of deliberation,
an intentional way of softly looking
at one's inside and outside.

This is about the healing gaze.

This is about swimming within the looking glass.

Let us begin.

NATURE OF SELF

Some people have a sense of a true self.
Some people feel they're always evolving,
always changing, that the self remains fluid.
What is the self to you, and how would
you describe your own personhood?

WORD INCEPTION

Scan the column of letters.
Which is the first that catches your eye?
Write down the first word you think of that begins
with this letter. On a separate piece of paper,
write down what the word makes you feel,
or use it as the title of a story.

200 FT.	# E	1
100 FT.	## F P	2
70 FT.	### T O Z	3
50 FT.	L P E D	4
40 FT.	P E C F D	5
30 FT.	E D F C Z P	6

---

25 FT.	F E L O P Z D	7
20 FT.	D E F P O T E C	8

---

15 FT.	L E F O D P C T	9
13 FT.	F D P L T C E O	10
10 FT.	P E Z O L C F T D	11

FEAR FRONT

This portly bunny is not the hare from Aesop's
The Hare & The Tortoise. Rather, it's one of the
timid ones from *The Hares & The Frogs*.
These hares frightened easily, until they stumbled
upon the frogs, who hid from them.
Write down the one great fear you have,
and how you can overcome this fear.

LIKENESS EFFECT

You are in a large room, with no doors.
One entire wall is a mirror, from ceiling to floor.
It is a looking glass. You look into it, and
see three people standing beside you.
Who are they?

INJURED FEELINGS

You stare harder at the looking glass.
It is changing its colours. It now transports you
to the moment your trust was broken.
What was this moment?

SOLE AGENCY

The tortoise is nowhere to be found
in this book's reauthoring of Aesop's fables.
What we do have is this baby sea turtle.
Insert the baby sea turtle into the original tale
of *The Hare & The Tortoise*, the one where the
hare loses the race. Write your version of the story.
What does the baby sea turtle do,
what is its role, and how does it all end?

SACRED KEEPSAKES

The tortoise is back, but this is a different tortoise.
It is the one in Aesop's fable of *The Tortoise & The Ducks*.
The fable starts off with this aphorism:
'The Tortoise, you know, carries his house on his back.
No matter how hard he tries, he cannot leave home.'
What are the most precious things you
keep close to you? What are these things
of great personal importance?

PRIVATE PLEDGE

This is a game of possibility.
Within the looking glass, you play hopscotch,
and land on one number. That number will be the
number of promises you decide to make to yourself.
Write down these promises.

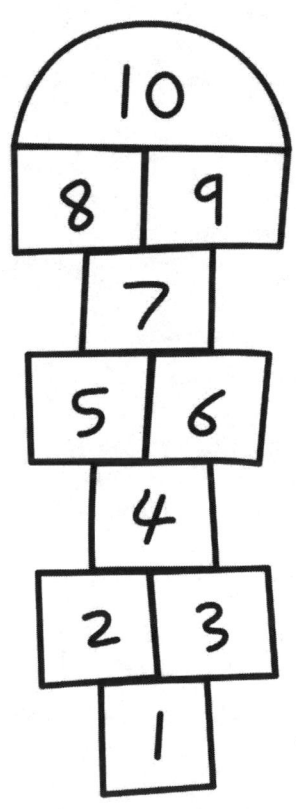

SOUL INSIGHT

X-rays give us a view of the insides
of things, sometimes even us.
If you could capture a radiograph of
your soul, what would you see?

CLEAN SLATE

In the Aesop fable, *The Fox & The Grapes*,
the fox can never jump high enough.
Some things simply remain beyond our reach.
There's no point beating ourselves up over it, or worse,
being left with the resentment and envy of the fox.
What is the one thing you've always desired,
the one thing which you've now realized
you're probably never going to have?
What will it take to move on,
to finally let go of that desire?

TWIN FLAME

The romantic in us likes to think
there's a soulmate waiting for us out there.
That we can spend a lifetime searching
for that ideal love, our perfect companion.
What are the qualities you imagine
would make up this other half?
What does your twin flame look like?

AN ABOMINATION

See no evil. Hear no evil. Speak no evil.
We wish we could be this virtuous,
to be such upstanding persons.
What is the most wicked thing you've been witness to?
Choose the nastiest of the lot.

FOUR BLEMISHES

We are all swans, and we all remain
the ugly ducklings of our own undoing.
We are all marked by little imperfections.
What are four imperfections that you notice
about your self? Jot them down, and
decide what you want to do with these traits.

BEING BLIND

Answer True or False: 'I know what I don't know.'
Explore what you mean by your response.

_____

_____

_____

_____

_____

_____

_____

_____

_____

_____

_____

_____

_____

WISE DEFERENCE

In the Aesop fable, *The Oak & The Reeds*, pride takes
a beating, when the oak tree is felled by the wind.
With their humility, the reeds endure, at story's end.
Write about moments where you would choose
the path of yielding, rather than resisting.
Write about the why.

DOWN THE LINE

Many things can happen in a decade.
Write a letter to your future self ten years from now.

FORCE OF METAPHOR

Look at the four peonies. The peony may take on
various meanings, including romance, honour, wealth,
and compassion. The symbolic language of flowers is wildly
interesting, and can translate into myriad sentiments.
If you could be a flower,
what flower would you choose to be?
The flower doesn't have to exist.
You can make it up, and write it into being.

FIRST STIRRINGS

The frogs are usually given a hard time
in Aesop's fables. Here's a really handsome frog.
He's the Frog Prince, after all.
Write about your first crush,
or the first time you fell in love.

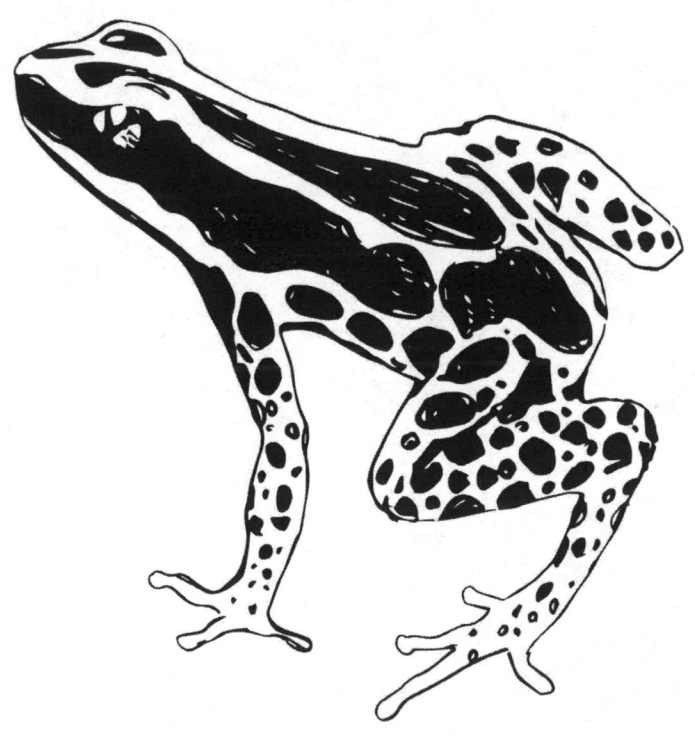

ALTERNATE WORLD

The looking glass turns opaque. It has become
a door that opens out into another world.
It is a free space, where all things can happen.
You walk through the door into this space.
What do you see around you?

GIVING SPIRIT

Within the large room suddenly appears ten windows.
Each window shows you a moment
when you were exceptionally kind.
List the ten moments.

EARLY MEMORY

The looking glass lifts itself off the wall,
and wafts in the air like a soft blanket.
You drape it over yourself, for a good night's sleep.
The blanket fills itself with tender images of
your childhood. Describe these images.

SECOND HOME

This beautiful shop on the corner of the street
has been entrusted to you. It is now yours.
What do you do with it?
What do you fill it up with?
How do you deck it up, put it to good use?
Describe how you would make
this quaint space uniquely yours.

OLD LONGINGS

When we are young, we build a life filled
with dreams and ambitions. Life, however, usually
serves up a heavy dose of reality, and suddenly
our early aspirations seem to dissolve.
Write down eight things you wish you'd done.
Circle three of them, and decide how
you're going to make them happen.

1.

2.

3.

4.

5.

6.

7.

8.

GRATITUDE TALLY

It's good to look back on the life we have lived.
It's good to take a moment to be grateful for
the small and the big things. You are going to pen
a thank-you note, as a list poem.
Write down twenty-five things to be thankful for.

1.

2.

3.

4.

5.

6.

7.

8.

9.

10.

11.

12.

13.

14.

15.

16.

17.

18.

19.

20.

21.

22.

23.

24.

25.

SHEDDING INERTIA

A jolt to normalcy is sometimes the best way
to get us out of our comfort zone.
Jot down five things you've seemed, perhaps
innocuously, to have become indifferent to.
Apathy often adds to the larger lethargy of life.
Decide which one of the five you'd like
to reignite interest in, and passion for.

CONSCIOUS DRAMA

Pick a farm animal for yourself.
Pick another farm animal for the one person
or thing you dislike. Write a story, where both of these
creatures are forced to interact with each other.

MINIMALIST ETHOS

The country mouse has gone home, and left
the city behind. The city was too fast, too flashy.
We live in a culture of bizarre excess.
We think more is more, and more is never enough.
Sometimes, it's good to take stock of just how much
we have. Write down seven things you own,
which you no longer have any use for.
If you can, give the items away to a friend,
or donate them. You can resell them too.
It's time to cut back on the excess.

1.

2.

3.

4.

5.

6.

7.

NEEDLESS BRUISING

The frog has returned, except it's now
an iridescent frog. It will let you fill in its colours.
This frog comes from the family in Aesop's
The Boys & The Frogs. It was terrified, but brave.
It had the courage to say it like it is:
That your idea of a good time
might result in someone else's pain.
Have you unintentionally caused someone hurt?
What colours will your frog be cloaked in?

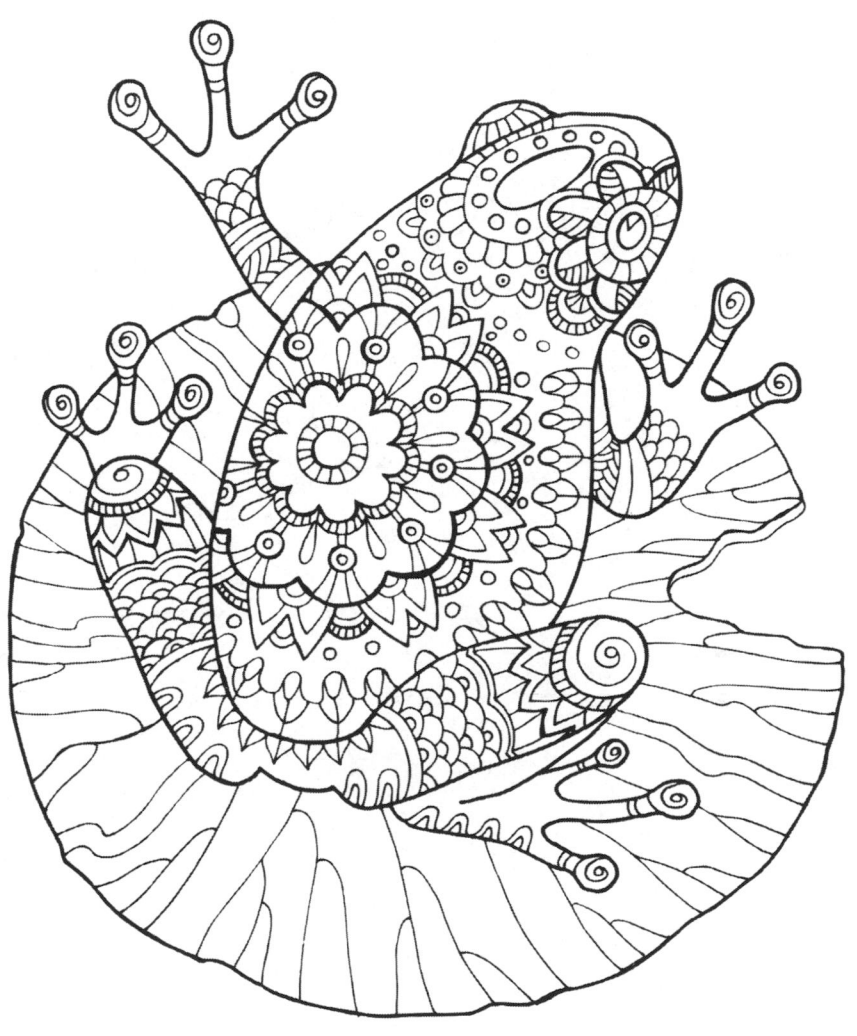

SWEET ESCAPE

This is a triptych.
The three panels obscure the
three things you try not to think about.
You find yourself running away,
or trying to forget them.
What are these three things?

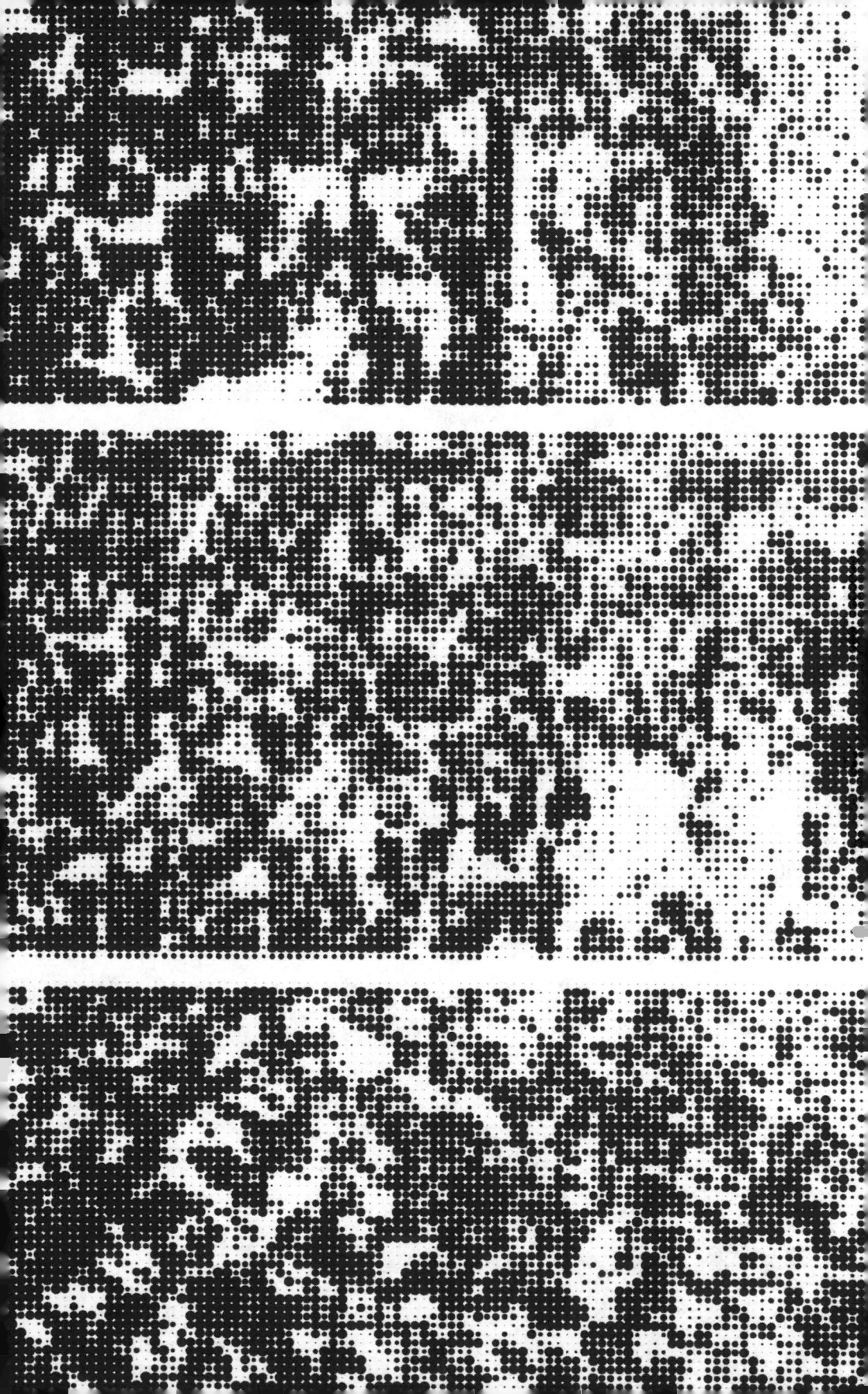

NEW NARRATIVE

The octopus has freed itself from Aesop
and the fisherman. Write your own fable,
featuring the majestic, mysterious creature.
What situation will it find itself in?
What moral dilemma? How will it all turn out?
Give the octopus its new coat of colours.

QUIET THOUGHT

You have a bird's eye view of everything from up here.
You are high up, and from here, you can see
everything for what it is. You have the wisdom of
a philosopher. Describe this clarity you see.

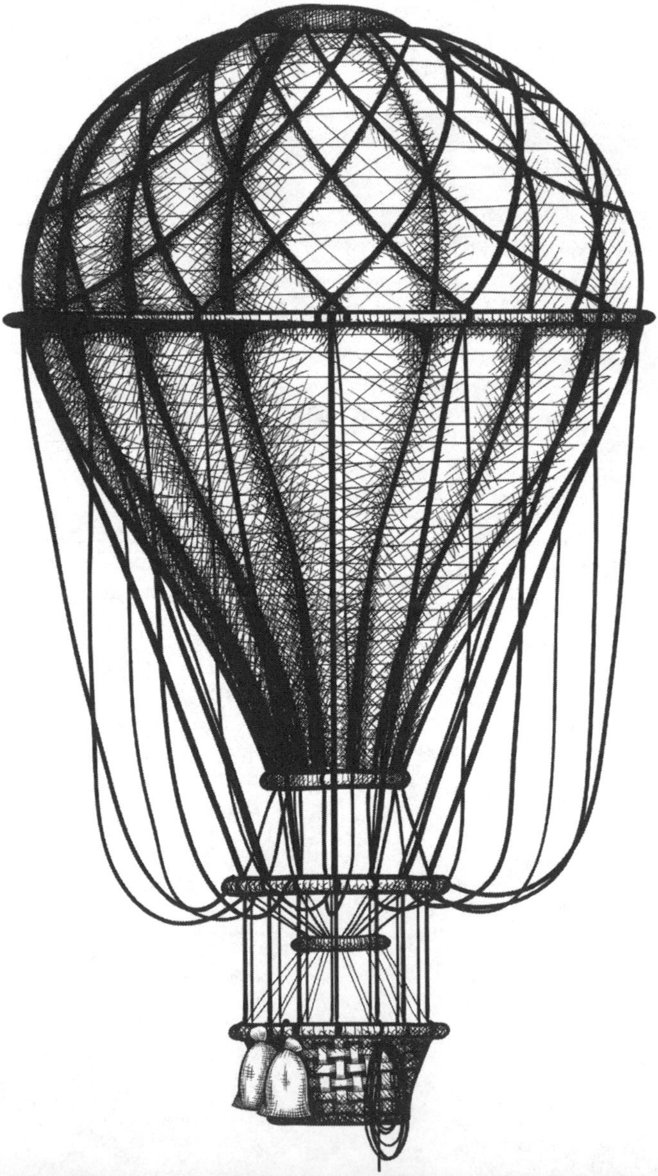

FINEST ATTRIBUTE

It's near impossible to find two snowflakes
exactly alike. It's a one in a million trillion chance
of that ever happening, according to science.
Choose your own favourite snowflake.
That snowflake represents the best thing about you.
What is this quality that you most value in your self?

BIG REVEAL

The looking glass has spread itself out, consuming
every bit of wall and ceiling and floor of the room.
You are standing in the middle of it.
Write down something about yourself
that absolutely no one knows about.

LOVE CONFESSION

The walls of the room turn to water.
The looking glass has run itself into the ground,
forming a perfectly round pond.
You look over its edge, into the still water.
For a moment, you become Narcissus,
yet your reflection has the ashen face of Echo.
Write a love letter to yourself.
Write it in the exact words you wish your lover
would conceive of a love profession.

PERSONAL BLISS

This is the love path you take, on the way
to paradise, your idea of happy heaven.
Describe this perfect place.
Describe your own vision of utopia.

These are Dr Eichelberger's parting remarks.

The looking glass is everywhere. It is all around you.
There is no room; yet, the room remains
every room you've ever been in.

This is the irony that intimates,
through every metaphor and allegory across these pages.
How they percolate to the surface of the lake.

As Carl Jung would have astutely said:
'A dream is a small hidden door in the deepest
and most intimate sanctum of the soul, which opens
up to that primeval cosmic night that was the soul,
long before there was the conscious ego.'

The fox is long gone,
and Freud's couch is once again empty.
The hare is having tea with the tortoise on the patio.

This has been a day of small epiphanies,
the soft realizations that help us frame our selves,
and know a bit more about where we are.
What follows is only possibility,
and often, a sense of arrival and gratitude.

It is evening. The sky is starting to fill with stars.
There, the looking glass is at it again.

Look at its glint, and inner light.
Look at how it hangs upon everything.

One day, in retrospect, the years of struggle
will strike you as the most beautiful.

Freud

ACKNOWLEDGEMENTS

My heartfelt thanks to:

The awesome Gaurav Shrinagesh, Nora Nazerene Abu Bakar, Rajni George, Ishani Bhattacharya and the team at Penguin Random House SEA for believing in my work, and bringing this book to life.

The Arts House, Ministry of Education, Nanyang Technological University, National Arts Council, National Library Board, Poetry Festival Singapore, Singapore Book Council, Sing Lit Station, and the University of Canberra for the support and opportunities over the years, where I was able to explore or share the importance of writing as a healing art.

The lovely artists whose beautiful works grace these pages. Your art is nothing short of stunning.

Arthur Dyck, Bradley J. Malkovsky, Brian E. Daley, Cate Marvin, Cheryl Giles, Cornelius Eady, Diana L. Eck, Don Share, Donald Swearer, Dorothy A. Austin, Francis X. Clooney, Janet Sylvester, John Wilkinson, Joseph Dan, Joyelle McSweeney, Kimberley Patton, Kwok Pui Lan, Michael Chiang, Nirmala PuruShotam, Orlando Menes, P. Oktor Skjaervo, Patrick Provost-Smith, Steve Tomasula, Steven Cramer, Theodore M. Hesburgh, Valerie Sayers. Thank you for your scholarship. Your guidance was invaluable.

Aaron Lee, Aaron Maniam, Adan Jimenez, Alvin Pang, Amanda Chong, Ami Kaye, Amy Gerstler, Annabelle Fabia-de Arroz, Aubrie Cox, Averyl Christine Rodrigues, Azira Amran, Barrie Sherwood, Boey Kim Cheng, Bryan Borland, C. E. Lukather, Carolyn Kreiter-Foronda, Catherine Limpe Candano, Celena Oon, Celine Chow, Charlene Shepherdson, Chris Mooney-Singh, Christine Chia, Christopher Higgs, Claire Betita de Guzman, Clara Chow, Corey Mesler, Crispin Rodrigues, D. S. Martin, Damon Chua, Dan Feng, Dan Waber, Daniel Jernigan, Daren Shiau, Darian Leader, Daryl Lim Wei Jie, Daryl Qilin Yam, David Wong Hsien Ming, Deborah Emmanuel, Diane Apostolos-Cappadona, Diane Smith, Divya Victor, Edwin Thumboo, Esther Vincent Xueming, Euginia Tan, Eva Lim, Felicia Low-Jimenez, Felix Cheong, Fiona Sze-Lorrain, Fong Hoe Fang, Foo Yueh Peng, Frank Stewart, Gabriel Sawicki, Gene Tan, Geraldine Song, Gregory Shushan, Gwee Li Sui, Hamid Roslan, Hedy Habra, Heng Siok Tian, Ho Kin Yunn, Iain Lim, Ian Chung, Jack Xi, Jacob Silkstone, Janice Holden, Jason Erik Lundberg, Jean Hair, Jeffrey Long, Jendi Reiter, Jenny Boully, Jerrold Yam, Jessica Faleiro, Jia Han Tong Chloe, Jocelyn Lau, Joey Chin, Johnmichael Simon, Jon Gresham, Joseph Stanton, Josephine Chia, Joses Ho, Joshua Ip, Joyce Cheng, Ju-Lyn Tan, Justin Deimen, Kemlyn Tan Bappe, Kenny Chan, Kenny Leck, Kevin Martens Wong, Kimberly Williams, Kirpal Singh, Koh Jee Leong, Koh Tai Ann, Krishna Udayasankar, Kristie

Ng, Kristine Ong Muslim, Lauren Camp, Laurin Bellg, Lee Tzu Pheng, Lee Wei Fen, Lee Yew Leong, Leong Liew Geok, Lily Hoang, Lim Siew Yea, Lisa Lip, Lo Hwei Shan, Low Kian Seh, Lydia Kwa, Mandy Pannett, Marc Nair, Margaret Devadason, Martha Silano, Mary-Ann Russon, Max Pasakorn, May Tan, Mayo Uno Martin, Megan M. Garr, Michael Linnard, Michael Ryan, Michele Thompson, Michelle Heng, Michelle Loh, Migs Bravo-Dutt, Muhamed Leoaidil, Neil Murphy, Neil Shepard, Ng Kah Gay, Ng Yi-Sheng, Nicole Kay, Nnorom Azuonye, Noah Eli Gordon, Noelle Q. de Jesus, Nuraliah Norasid, O Thiam Chin, Olivia Ho, Ovidia Yu, Ow Yeong Wai Kit, Patricia Karunungan, Patricia Matsueda, Paul Tan, Phan Ming Yen, Phil Brown, Pierre Vinclair, Pooja Nansi, Randy Brooks, Ranga Chandrarathne, Rajeev S. Patke, Richard Collins, Robert McDowell, Robert Yeo, Robin Hemley, Rodrigo Dela Peña Jr., Rosemarie Somaiah, Rosemary Chan, S. Brent Plate, S. Mickey Lin, Sadiah Boonstra, Samara Cahill, Samuel Caleb Wee, Sarah Tan Shu Ling, Savinder Kaur, Sean Moreland, Shamimah Mujtaba, Sharon Lim, Shelly Bryant, Shilpa Dikshit Thapliyal, Shirley Chew, Siah Sheng Yuan, Stella Kon, Stephanie Dogfoot, Stephanie Ye, Sueyuen Juliette Lee, Suffian Hakim, Sung Do Song, Susan Antolin, Susan M. Schultz, Tan Puay Shian, Tara Dhar Hasnain, Thaddeus Rutkowski, Timothy Liu, Toh Hsien Min, Topaz Winters, Tse Hao Guang, Uma Maheswari d/o Nallathambi, Verena Tay, William Phuan, William Wan, Yeow Kai Chai, Yong Shu Hoong, Zafar Anjum. Thank you for our previous collaborations, no matter how small. Thank you so much for your creative energy. Many of you have offered encouragement, support, and/or previous insight into my work, and for that, I am deeply appreciative.

Alicia Guarracino, Brenna Casey, Daniel Citro, Emily DiFilippo, Grant Osborn, Iris Law, Jaclyn Dwyer, Jared Randall, Jarett Haley, Jessica Martinez English, Justin Perry, Kristen Eliason, Michael Valente, Monica Mody, Rachael Hsiao-Shih Lee, Raul Jara, Rebecca Cheung, Ryan Downey, Ryan Glenn Smith, Sami Schalk, Silpa Swarnapuri, Stephanie White, Susan Blackwell Ramsey, Tasha Matsumoto, Veronica Fitzpatrick. Thank you for those splendid conversations and workshops all those years ago.

Amy, Ben, Benji, Chee Keong, Cheh, Corinne, Ems, Eric, Jackie, Jenny, Jess, Jin, Karen, Leonard, Lilen, Lynn, Mel, Ming, Nit, Paul, Pee, Poh Yoke, Rajesh, Ramani, Richard, Shil, Veronica, Wan Yhim, Ying Yew, and my best bud Rob. For the years and friendship.

My students, many of whom have become fond friends and gone on to do amazing things. Thank you for the beautiful discourse and keeping me on my toes.

My parents and family for always being there. Much love to The Soong Sisters from Guan Jia, and all the baby sea turtles on the sandbank!

Eric F. Tinsay Valles, the most awesome godfather anyone could have.

F. X. For your prayers. *Amor est spiritus qui nos alet.* Indeed, love is the breath that sustains us.

Above all, God, for the infinite love and mercy—and the grace of a blessed life.